Leopold & Martha

Little Kennebec Press

ISBN: 978-0-578-90165-7

Northern Flicker Nest Box diagram is courtesy of the US Forest Service.
https://www.fs.fed.us/t-d/pubs/htmlpubs/htm00712847/images/draw.pdf

All illustrations by Catherine Allis.
Book design by Lauren Berg at www.botanicmagic.studio

Printed by Ingramspark, United States of America.

First printing, 2021.

*Little
Kennebec
Press*

Little Kennebec Press
236 W. Kennebec Rd.
Machias, ME 04654

Leopold & Martha

written & illustrated by Catherine Allis

For Aiden, Landen, John Samuel,
Esther & Josiah

This book is dedicated to my mother,
Barbara S. Trenis, for her constant
encouragement & to my husband,
John, for all his support.

Mimi and Grah

lived in a cedar house
nestled among the ancient pines

in the

Black Forest

of   Colorado.

The trees sheltered pigmy nuthatches, chickadees, pine siskins and woodpeckers. Many unusual birds enjoyed the safety of these tall old trees as they migrated spring and fall. Mimi kept seed and suet there for them every day so the birds knew they could always find a meal.

Right before they moved in to their Black Forest home, Mimi brought a friend by to see it. Just as they drove by, a bird flew right out of a hole in the front of the house. "What was that?" asked her friend, Joan. She and Mimi began to snicker. That night Mimi told Grah about the bird. Grah just raised his eyebrows but he didn't say a word.

"What was a bird doing in our new house? thought Mimi.

Mimi and Grah moved in and settled into life in the Black Forest. There was no sign of a hole in the house. Life was peaceful with birds all around.

Grah and his sons built a barn with a wood shop. He installed a woodstove with a long pipe that went all the way through the top of the barn! Grah liked to build boats and had a design already in his mind as they finished the barn. He put all of those plans on paper and set up his barn to build that boat. Grah bought wood and screws, clamps and glue.

He started working
right away.

That winter the wind blew and it

snowed

and

snowed

in the Black Forest.

Their first Christmas in the little cedar house would be full of children.

Grah and Mimi drove to the National Forest to cut a nice tall tree. Mimi decorated it with strings of lights and placed the ornaments just so. Packages were in place and the house smelled of Christmas when the children arrived. Grandchildren, eyes wide with delight, sampled cookies and cocoa...

...and talked of Santa finding them deep in the forest.

In the mornings, the children
helped Mimi fill the feeders with
seed and watched the birds enjoy
her suet.

Grah and Mimi's sons cross country skied every day. They marveled
at the boat beginning to take shape in Grah's barn. Their daughter
bundled her boys in heavy snow suits and sent them out to sled.
She always found them helping Grah with his boat building in the
warm barn.

It was a
Christmas
the children
would
always
remember.

Once the holidays were over,
Mimi and Grah returned to quiet
days. Their home was warm and cozy
through those long months though the
winds blew snow and hoarfrost covered
the trees.

April dawned, but winter held her grip. One morning, early in the
month, Mimi and Grah heard something drilling on the chimney
pipe. They looked at each other. They heard a high pitched bird call.
It went on and on! Grah said, "That's a woodpecker!"

Mimi said,
"That's Leopold!"

Mimi had been feeding the
birds all winter and had come
to know a few of them personally!
Leopold is a Northern Flicker.

He and his mate, Martha, spend the winters deep in the forest.
Mimi had seen them in the wind-blown areas of the yard looking
for insects and had often watched them at her suet feeder.

April is the time Leopold begins to look for a nesting spot for
Martha. Leopold had decided long ago that Mimi and Grah's little
cedar house was just right. He called out in his high pitched trill
as he flew into one of their tall, tall pines.

In early April,
Leopold began

'drilling'

on the metal
chimney pipe
to show off
for Martha.

Within the next two weeks he
would find what he thought to be
the perfect spot for Martha, right in
the wall of Mimi and Grah's little cedar
house! He could drill out a hole in hours.

Grah and Mimi were envisioning their beautiful cedar house
looking like a Swiss cheese! Mimi would go out and fuss at Leopold.
But, before the day was done, he would have a good three-inch hole
drilled in one of the walls of their house.

Grah came home from work, put up the big ladder and repaired
the hole. Every few days Leopold found a new spot and every evening
Grah would come home and patch it up.

Leopold
was getting
desperate!

He had to
have a home
for Martha.

Finally, Grah and Mimi decided what they'd do.

Grah came home from work the next day with cedar boards, some screws and a bag of fresh wood shavings. He built a beautiful cedar box with a three-inch hole in the top front. He mounted it right over Leopold's hole on the west wall of the house, then painted it to match.

He filled it
with the
fresh wood
shavings

and put the
finishing
touches on
the box late
on April 30th.

Early the next morning Mimi saw Leopold
pulling out shavings and throwing them
far below to the ground.

He and Martha moved in that very morning. Grah and Mimi
could hear the birds pecking inside the box from inside their
house. Martha laid her eggs and the pecking continued. Mimi just
grinned, "Listen, Grah. They're busy!" Grah was happy, too. Every
morning they listened to the steady pecking and wondered
what in the world those birds were doing. Would they peck
through the wall of their house?

One evening in May, Mimi was working in her garden. She
looked up and there was Leopold, his head just out of the hole,
"Look, Grah!" said Mimi, "Leopold is enjoying the sunset!" Grah
just smiled, "I suppose he is."

They didn't
see Martha
for a couple
of weeks.
She was

sitting

on

her

eggs.

Soon the baby woodpeckers
hatched and Martha and Leopold
were busy.

Martha seemed to enjoy being out in the fresh air again looking for insects. She and Leopold worked together to keep the little ones fed. Soon Mimi realized the pecking had stopped. Grah said it looked like the flickers had moved out.

The babies had flown, and Martha and Leopold were busy teaching them to find ants and beetles in the grassy fields. Mimi and Grah often saw them in the yard and heard them calling.

They would learn to shelter in
the deep forest by fall.

The children visited again in the summer
and were delighted to see the young flickers
searching for insects

in

the

grass!

Grah took the box down to
clean it out for next year.
"Look Mimi," He said, "It's clean
as a whistle!"

The birds had left it spotless. Mimi and Grah discovered what
all the pecking was. Leopold and Martha had carved out a nice
smooth rounded area right in the bottom of the box. The birds
worked and worked. Mimi and Grah knew they had liked their
house.

The next April Mimi heard Leopold drumming on the chimney
pipe again. "Grah" she said, "Leopold's showing off for Martha."

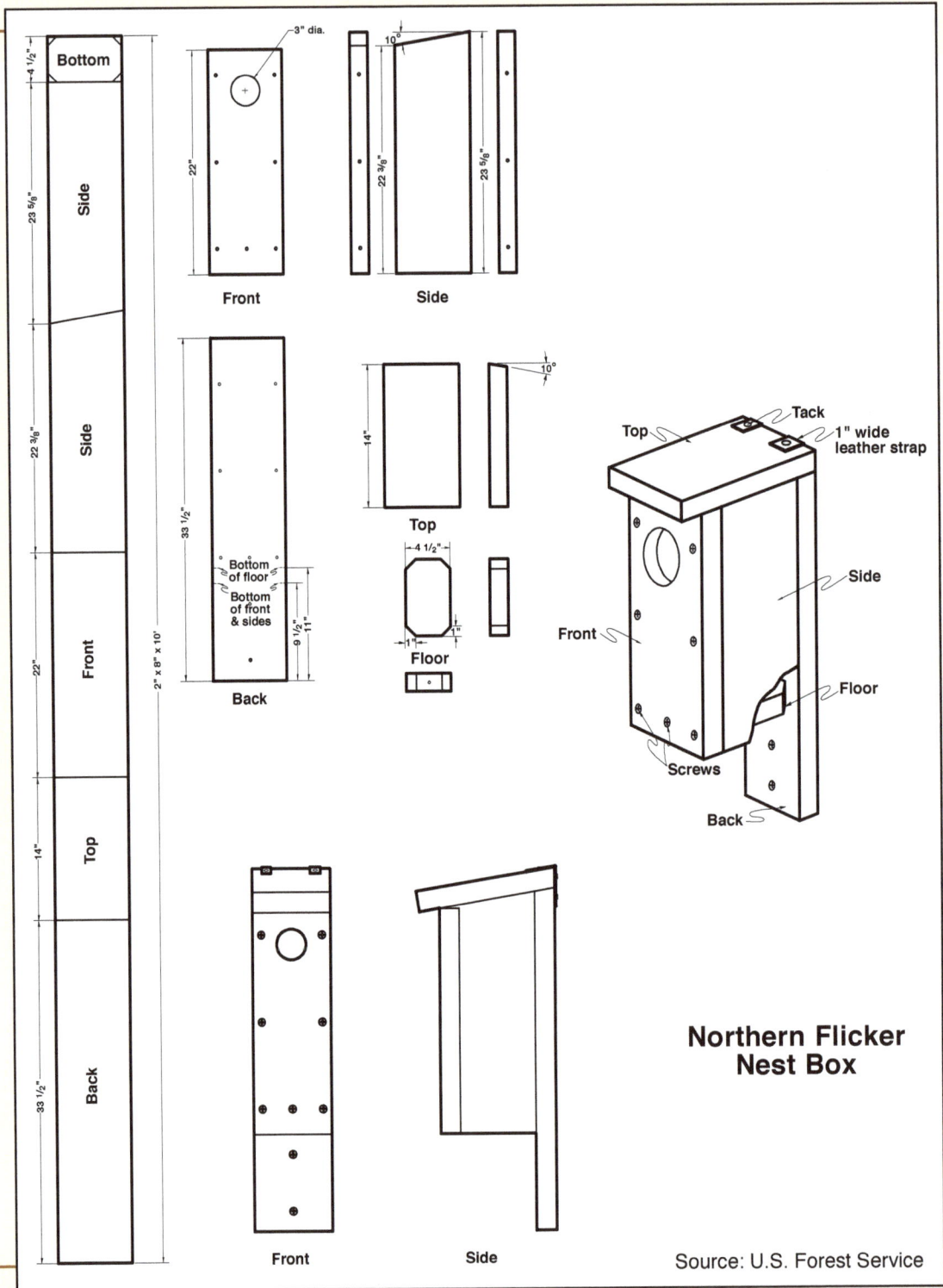

"We'd better get that

box ready!"

Northern Flicker
Nest Box

THE END